ENGLISH
THROUGH
POETRY

The Alemany Press

ENGLISH
THROUGH
POETRY

by Mary Ann Christison

illustrations by

KATHLEEN B. PETERSON

The Alemany Press
P.O. Box 5265
San Francisco, Ca. 94101

ISBN 0-88084-002-1

The Alemany Press
P.O. Box 5265
San Francisco, Ca. 94101

ii

To Carrie

OTHER TITLES OF INTEREST

CHRISTISON, M.A. and BASSANO, S.
Look Who's Talking

DENNIS, J.M., GRIFFIN, S. and WILLS, R.
English Through Drama

FORD, C and SILVERMAN, A.
American Cultural Encounters

MACULAITIS, J.D. and SCHERAGA, M.
What to do Before the Books Arrive (and after)

OLSEN, J. E. W-B
Communication Starters and Other Activities

OLSEN, R. E. W-B
American Business Encounters

Acknowledgements

I would like to express my gratitude to Barbara Justesen for her assistance in typing the manuscript, to Sharron Bassano for her comments on an earlier draft of this book, to Dr. Karl Krahnke for the correspondence on theory and methodology which has kept me creating and producing, to Professor Barbara M. Hales for her wonderful poetry, to Roger Olsen for his patience and professional support, to Kathy Peterson for her delightful illustrations, to Kim and Cameron Christison for their constant encouragement, and, of course, to my students who make it all so enjoyable and worthwhile.

TABLE OF CONTENTS

CHAPTER ONE

Using Poetry in ESL

Our class is like a garden
And we are flowers there
Each has a rare, special beauty
For all who come here to share.

            by an advanced level ESL student

CHAPTER ONE

Using Poetry in ESL

Introduction

There are many reasons for incorporating poetry in the ESL class. It is an excellent way to improve reading skills, develop more vocabulary and nuture a love of words and sounds in adults and children alike, an idea which provides a firm foundation on which to build more advanced language skills later on. A student who enjoys the language first is well on the way to success in any program. Students can read and enjoy short poems in English when they do not possess the language skills to tackle longer more complicated pieces of prose. A carefully chosen poem which appeals to students' interests and meets their emotional and psychological needs can, when used correctly, build self-confidence and encourage personal/individual expression at a very early stage in the language learning process. Through poetry, students seem to see, hear, and feel something that prose cannot express.

Despite the many advantages of using poetry in the ESL classroom, many teachers never use it. They are afraid of it, they don't know how to use it, or perhaps they were turned off by poetry themselves at some point in their educational experience . This is a sad occurrence and all too common. Looking back on our own experiences, we can probably identify with these feelings. Have you ever sat through a class where poetry was presented in a dreary and un-interesting manner? Did you talk about what poetry is? Did you take it apart piece by piece, step by step?

Poetry isn't meant to be dissected. It is first meant to be read and enjoyed! Students don't need to learn about meters, rhyme schemes, cadence, balance, etc. in order to enjoy poetry. After all, who says that a poem even has to have those things. It doesn't. And besides, we really don't know what poetry is. The only thing we really know about poetry is what it should do and how it should make us feel. These are the important things.

Eleanor Farjeon's poem entitled "Poetry" summarizes the idea quite nicely:

> What is Poetry? Who knows
> Not a rose, but the scent of the rose;
> Not the sky, but the light in the sky;
> Not the fly, but the gleam of the fly;
> Not the sea, but the sound of the sea;
> Not myself, but what makes me
> See, hear, and feel something that prose
> Cannot: and what it is, who knows?

Lee Bennett Hopkins pointed out in his book, Pass the Poetry Please, a very interesting concept about poetry which is especially applicable for the ESL teacher. He said that poetry is the only art that works most frequently with second-hand materials. By this statement he means that although poems occasionally create new words or new combinations, they most often draw their vocabulary from the same source as everyone else. The words appearing in poetry can be found in telephone conversations, grocery lists, homework assignments, final examinations, store advertisements, road signs, etc.

In other words, they can be found everywhere!
Essentially, a carefully chosen poem contains much of
the vocabulary students will use in real-life situations. The ideas expressed in poetry are not so far
from a student's own life. Poetry is not something
meant for other generations or times. Through the
sharing and discussion of a poem, our students can be
made to realize this. However, in order to accomplish
this goal, the poetry must first stimulate them to
share and discuss. That is why it is important to
develop criteria for the selection of the poetry in
the ESL class.

Criteria for Selection

1. High student interest. It is important to
choose poetry which is appealing and to which most
students can relate. Students will not be stimulated
to express their own ideas unless they are interested
in the topic. They must identify with the poetry
they are exposed to. It must mean something to them
personally. The quality of their experience will be
related to the kind of poetry which is offered to
them. With today's wealth of poetry from which to
choose there is no excuse for bringing poetry into
the classroom which does not give true meaning to our
students and the world in which they live, their
everyday world.

This point is best illustrated with poems which
have been favorites of a number of our ESL students.
For high school students try "Street Song" by Myra
Cohn Livingston.

> O, I have been walking
> with a bag of potato chips
> me and potato chips
> munching along.

Walking along
eating potato chips
big old potato chips
crunching along,

Walking along
munching potato chips
me and potato chips
lunching along.

Bring potato chips or similar snacks in small
packages to class. Talk about tastes, which ones
they like best, what sounds they make when they are
eaten, and how they are made, to name a few ideas.
It is also fun to find out when they eat the snacks.
Compare answers. Not every student will feel the
same. The poem could also key a whole discussion on
snacking, eating habits and customs in their own
countries. This type of experience is appealing and
holds high student interest because the students have
something they can relate to.

For young children "Recipe" by Bobbi Katz has
been successful.

I can make a sandwich
I can really cook
I made up this recipe
That should be in a book.
Take a jar of peanut butter
Give it a spread,
Until you have covered
A half a loaf of bread.
Pickles and pineapple,
Strawberry jam
Salami and bologna
And 1/2 a pound of ham--
Pour some catsup on it.

Mix in the mustard well.
It will taste delicious
If you don't mind the smell.

Bring the food to class and have them make
sandwiches. Follow up with an activity where
they explain how they made the sandwich. Talk
about likes and dislikes and how things smell
and taste. There are innumerable activities
which key off of this one simple poem.

Poetry has also been successful with older
students. Non-academic adults have enjoyed
"Money" by Richard Armour.

Workers earn it,
Spendthrifts burn it,
Bankers lend it,
Women spend it,
Forgers fake it,
Taxes take it,
Dying leave it,
Heirs receive it,
Thrifty save it,
Misers crave it,
Robbers seize it,
Rich increase it,
Gamblers lose it
I could use it.

Following an introduction of this poem
talk about money. Bring money to class. What
money you use, of course, depends on what the
students need. Refugees in the United States
would have to learn U. S. currency while
foreign students studying in Britain would
have another need. Give students practice in
shopping and buying things by bringing empty

packages to class (cereal boxes, coffee cans, etc.). Have
them take some money and a list of things to get. They
should find the items, pay for them, make change, etc. A
follow-up exercise may be taking them to the local supermarket. Have them assist you with your own shopping by
dividing up the list or have them shop for a class party.
This is a good experience because they plan the menu and
must buy the items with the money they have collected.
The poem introduces useful and interesting vocabulary and
all on the subject of money.

There are a number of additional activities which can
be implemented to assure comprehension. Have students do
role-playing activities with the money. One student can
be a gambler, another a robber, miser, banker, forger, and
a spendthrift. Ask the students to act out what they do
with the money and have the class guess what role they are
playing. Another idea would be to give them play money
and have them tell you what they would buy with it.

Foreign students in academic preparation programs
enjoy poems from "The Math Battle" by Stephen Silberam.

> Cubes are swirling through my head
> Pi's attack me in my bed.
> How much to carry? How much to keep?
> Circles everywhere, radii too
> In my brain--a number zoo!

Have students who have math backgrounds draw the
examples on the board and explain the new vocabulary.
This not only provides an excellent way for them to learn
vocabulary, but makes the students more responsible for
their own learning. Once they discover enough about each
other, they continually share information, a method which
feels good and right from the standpoint of both the
learner and the teacher.

2. Short and Simple. It has been said that the shorter the poem, the longer the thought. Where poetry for ESL students is concerned this is particularly sound advice. Poetry which is direct and to the point makes it memorable, easy to remember and hard to forget--qualities which are much needed in the language class. Avoid poetry with excessive idioms and unusual vocabulary. These will all have to be taught and discussed. Two or three new items make it fun, but many more make it too difficult for the students.

A favorite short and simple poem has been "Kitten" by Ogden Nash.

> The trouble with a kitten is
> THAT
> Eventually it becomes a
> CAT.

Consider this poem and those in the preceding section. They are all short, simple, and direct, containing common everyday language the students would use in real-life situations. Poetry could, for more advanced students, be considerably longer than the Nash poem and others in this chapter. But even with advanced classes, it is a good idea to keep the length of the poems to a minimum.

3. Fun-filled and rhythmic. Experience has taught us that language learners enjoy easy rhymes, aliteration, quick action and the humor much poetry contains. Poems which contain these qualities make a lasting impression on language learners. For example, not longer after presenting Richard Armour's poem "Money," students started their own rhymes. The following were written by intermediate level ESL students.

```
Children play in it
Hippos stay in it
              (Mud)

Plants need it
Worms feed on it
              (Dirt)

Crackers need it
To mice
We feed it
              (Cheese)
```

Give them a chance to use the rhythm in these poems to write their own poems. It will happen naturally. If the teacher enjoys the poem, rhythm, aliteration, etc., so will the students. The key is in the initial presentation in the class.

Criteria for Presentation

There is no trickery involved in reading poetry aloud. Lee Bennett Hopkins, in his book entitled Pass the Poetry, Please, suggests five guidelines which may be helpful. These guidelines have been adapted for use in the ESL class. They are for teachers and students because both will be reading poetry aloud and sharing their personal ideas.

1. Practice. Know the poem very well. Read it over and over, making clear the words you want to emphasize to others and the ideas you think are important.

2. Try to follow the natural rhythm of the poem. Sometimes the appearance of the poem on the printed page will give you an idea about what rhythm the author intended. Some poems are meant to be read

softly, others are meant to be lively and quick. Exaggerate the rhythm. After students have practiced in this manner, then tone it down.

3. Make pauses in the poem where you think they make sense; that is how we talk. Sometimes we say our words quickly, then we pause, collect our thoughts and go on again.

4. Speak in a natural voice. This makes it easy for people to listen to you. It is a good idea to exaggerate rhythm and aliteration where appropriate, but it should not be overdone.

5. After you are through with the poem, be quiet. Give your audience time to think. Let them talk if they want to. Do not demand responses. It will destroy the mood the poem has created.

CHAPTER TWO

Choral Readings

CHAPTER TWO
Choral Readings

Rationale

Even though students may understand the criteria
for the oral reading of poetry discussed in Chapter
One, such as practice, pauses, and rhythm, and
receive numerous examples and opportunities to
practice, they may still not be able to get up in
front of an audience and make their presentation
successfully. It seems all the criteria are met,
they have practiced, they like the poem, it is something they can identify with, it is short and fun-
filled. Something, however, is missing. They still
cannot relax and present it easily and with fluency.
The situation is common, but certainly need not be a
prolonged problem. One way to bridge the gap between
what students enjoy reading silently and what skills
they need to share with others, is to use choral
readings. This activity encourages students to relax
and provides them with the tools they need to share
poetry they enjoy with others. Choral Readings
encourage learners to have fun with the poetry
together.

The criteria for selecting poetry for choral
reading are basically the same as for selecting poetry
for the ESL classroom in general. These criteria are
carefully outlined in Chapter One.

Criteria for Presentation

The method for presenting choral readings will
vary from teacher to teacher. There is no specific

14

step-by-step method. Nevertheless, there are
several important points which should be kept in mind:

1. Give students time to read through the
choral reading silently first. Then, the teacher
should read it orally for the students. (Remember
the criteria for oral presentation.)

2. When there are unfamiliar words or
expressions, be sure to gloss them at the end of the
poem. How much glossing you do will depend on the
level of the students. Students need time to discuss
and ask questions about new vocabulary.

3. Let students volunteer for parts or groups.
If you don't have volunteers, then ask them to
participate in a group. If you have a mix of
English ability, it is a good idea to put the
beginner and the advanced in the same group, mix
them. They can then help and teach each other and
become less dependent on the teacher and more
reliant on their peers and their personal resources.

4. Have students say the line(s) after you first
rather than alone. There are several reasons for
this. First, they may naturally mimic your
enthusiasm and love of the poetry. It is catching!
If you like the poem and enjoy it, your students
will know and will respond to that. This attitude
develops the kind of atmosphere in the classroom
wherein students can feel confident and accepted in
sharing their ideas and opinions and, thus, in using
the language more effectively. Secondly, reinforce-
ment that they can perform successfully in a group
helps build self-confidence. They will become more
independent and participate later on without the
teacher's assistance.

5. If special skills are called for like chang-
the voice from high to low, give them a chance to
practice this. Be free, laugh, experiment, and
enjoy. That is what makes choral reading fun!
Exaggerate when possible and where appropriate.

6. Remember to get their attention. Use
"Clock" to introduce a lesson on time or "The
Umbrella Brigade" on a rainy day to talk about
weather. Bring umbrellas and clocks to class. Use
pictures. Ask questions and encourage them to give
their ideas and opinions. Choral Reading is only a
beginning, a tool for stimulating and developing
creative expression through language.

Reading 1

"The Umbrella Brigade"
by Laura E. Richards

Group 1:   "Pitter, patter!"
             falls the rain,

Group 2:   On the school-room window-pane,

Groups 1   Such a splashing! such a dashing!*
    & 2:

Group 3:   Will it ever be dry again?

Group 1:   Down the gutter moves a flood,

Group 2:   And the crossing's* deep in mud;

Group 3:   And the puddles! oh, the puddles

```
ALL:        Are a sight to stir one's blood!*

                    (PAUSE)

CHORUS:*

Group 1:    But let it rain

Group 2:    Tree-toads
 (HIGH)     and frogs

Group 3:    Muskets* and
 (MED)      Pitchforks,

Group 2:    Kittens
 (LOW)      and Dogs!

Group 1:    Dash away!  splash away!
            Who is afraid?

Group 2     Here we go
  & 3:

ALL:        The UMBRELLA BRIGADE
```

_____

Brigade: a group of people
Crossing: a sidewalk
Stir one's blood: to become afraid
Chorus: When it rains very, very hard we use the
         expressions in the chorus. Of course, it
         doesn't really rain cats, dogs, tree-
         toads, etc. It just rains very hard.

Reading 2

CLOCK
  by Valerie Worth

ALL: This clock
           has stopped

MED: Some gear
           Or spring
           Gone wrong - -

HIGH: Too tight

MED: Or cracked,

LOW: Or choked
           With dust;

             (PAUSE)

MED: A year
           Has passed
           Since last
           It said

HIGH: Ting ting

MED: Or tick

LOW: Or tock

ALL: Poor
           Clock

Reading 3

SUBWAYS ARE PEOPLE
By Lee Bennett Hopkins

ALL: Subways are people

Group 1:   People standing

Group 2:   People sitting

Groups 3   People swaying to and fro
& 4:

Group 3:   Some in suits

Group 4:   Some in tatters

Groups 1   People I will never know.
& 2:

Group 3:   Some with glasses
                Some without

Group 4:   Boy with smile
                Girl with frown

Group 1:   People dashing

Group 2:   Steel flashing

Groups 1   Up and down and
& 2:   'round the town

ALL: Subways are people - -

Group 1:   People old

Group 2:   People new

Groups 3   People always on the go
    & 4:

Group 3:   Racing

Group 4:   running,

Groups 3   rushing people
    & 4:

ALL: People I will never know.

CHAPTER THREE

Writing Poetry

We're writing poetry
    in class today.
I said, "Not me.
I don't want to stay."

But the teacher said try.
So I sit down to write
And you know, I discovered
I was really quite bright.

This poetry's easy
And before the hour was through
I wrote a little poem
That would please even you!

       by an advanced level ESL student

CHAPTER THREE
Writing Poetry

Once students have been exposed to and enjoyed poetry for a period of time, they naturally react positively to an offer to compose poems of their own. Language learners should be encouraged to write their own original verse. These activities build self-confidence in the students and create positive feelings about the language learning experience. Teachers must remember that students will most likely write about experiences which are deeply felt. Because the poetry is very personal, all honest efforts on the part of the students should be praised and encouraged. Their ideas, when expressed in words, will continue to live in their minds, hearts and memories forever.

What follows in this chapter is a brief introduction to several methods which have been used with success in ESL classes in getting students to write their own poetry.

Similes

A good method for getting students started in writing their own poetry is to use similes. Similes are figures of speech that compare two dissimilar things. The words <u>like</u> and <u>as</u> are used.

Begin by giving students phrases such as "as green

as _____," or "as good as
_____.' If they say <u>grass</u>
for the first example, have them brainstorm other
things that would fit the blank. There will probably
be a number of things in the classroom which would
work. Once students understand this comparison idea,
they can be led into other comparisons which are
slightly more advanced: "My friend is like _____,"
"My book is like _____," "The man is as
_____ as _____," or "She is
as _____ as _____." Write the
phrases on the board and have them brainstorm possibilities. ESL students at the advanced level came up
with these ideas:

> He is as tall as my friend Jim the
>   basketball player.
> She is as fat as the pumpkin I bought
>   at the store.
> The sky is as blue as my friend's
>   eyes.
> This is as much fun as an amusement
>   park.

Students will want a chance to share what they
have written with the class. You can have them do
this in a large group or divide them into small
groups or dyads. Giving learners the opportunity to
share their ideas starts them thinking in terms of
poetic imagery. Eventually, they will be able to use
these phrases in composing full-length poems of
their own.

In the beginning your students will probably
begin making comparisons at a very elementary level.
This may or may not have anything to do with their
skill in using the language. I have worked with
native speakers who have also begun writing poetry

at an elementary level. For example, consider the sentences written by the advanced level students cited above. The idea of comparing <u>tall</u> and a <u>basketball player</u> is certainly not new, nor is <u>fat</u> to <u>pumpkin</u>, <u>blue eyes</u> to the <u>blue sky</u>, or <u>fun</u> to an <u>amusement park</u>. These ideas, however, may be new to the students and may represent a whole new way of looking at things.

When your students begin writing at this level, accept what they have written, but continue to work with them. They need to develop additional ideas to eventually lead them into making their comparisons in a slightly more sophisticated way.

Consider the sentences below. They were also written by the same advanced level students sometime later. Notice that they have become more sophisticated in terms of their ability to use poetic imagery.

> He is tall and straight like the
> little toy soldier in my little
> brother's room.

> Her feet were too small for her
> body like the tiny table in your
> office piled high with many papers
> and books and much junk.

Both of these students were creating ideas and developing their ability to express themselves in a new way in a new language.

If your students have difficulty in understanding the concept of similes, here are two ideas with help. Give them pictures and have them find things the pictures have in common or bring a small number of objects to class and have them do the same. Begin with obvious pictures or objects, e.g., five pictures of animals or five white objects, then move to more difficult ones where students will have to search, think, and create, in order to identify what the objects or pictures have in common.

Elementary English, April, 1972, pp. 585-86, contains an article on similes entitled "Simile, Darn You, Simile," by Elaine Campbell Smith which will definitely provide inspiration on the value of similes. in the classroom and, in addition, give some useful ideas on activities for classroom use.

Haiku

This is another form of poetry which has been successful with ESL students. Haiku is very short and the form is easy to remember. It is a Japanese poetic form. There are three non-rhyming lines containing 17 syllables of five, seven, and five. It is best to use the form only as a suggestion. If there are 16 or 18 syllables, it makes no difference. The main idea is to motivate your students to express their thoughts in just a few words and give careful thought to which words will communicate their thoughts most effectively. The only real requirements are that true Haiku should relate to nature or the seasons of the year in some way and should capture a single moment or image in nature. A reader should be able to tell the season the Haiku poem is depicting from key words within the poem.

To introduce Haiku to your students read a variety of   poems to them. Find a small picture which depicts the images created in the poem and display it as you read the poem. Encourage the students to discuss the poem and the images.

It is a good idea to find pictures for each poem

you introduce. After the initial presentation of the poems and pictures and the short discussion, follow-up with another oral reading exercise where the students have to match the poem you read to the correct picture. This helps them focus in on the images the poems have created for them and serves as a good exercise in listening comprehension. You might then want to give each student a poem and have him/her find an appropriate picture to match the poem. Bring old magazines to class and have them do this as a class project. This activity has been used with very young children and adults and has been enjoyed by both. Make certain you go over each poem individually with the students. You read the lines and have them repeat after you, or for more confident students have them read the line first. The teacher corrects only words which were mispronounced. Let the student be expressive and independent. Answer any questions they may have about vocabulary.

Most students will want to share their pictures and poems with the class. Help them prepare for this experience in the following way.

1. Go over each poem individually with the students. Have them repeat the lines after you and then have them repeat the whole poem for you. Make certain they understand all the vocabulary. This can be done with each individual student while the rest of the class is looking for pictures to match their poems.

2. After all students have pictures and have worked with the teacher put them in dyads and have them share their poems with just one other person. Sharing with just one other person is not so frightening.

3. After you have given them a few minutes to share in pairs, put two pairs together and make groups of four. Have each person share in the small group of four as they did in pairs.

4. As a culminating activity, you could have them share in front of the large group. Using the procedure above provides a less threatening approach to the sharing of poetry. Sometimes it is not the language they are afraid of, but the idea of having to work individually in front of a large group.

There are many excellent books of Haiku poetry to choose from. The ones which have worked best in ESL classes are the following:

Beilenson, Peter (trans.) Japanese Haiku. The Peter Pauper Press, 1956.
Beilenson, Peter (trans.) The Four Seasons. The Peter Pauper Press, 1958.
Beilenson, Peter and H. Behn. (trans.) Haiku Harvest. The Peter Pauper Press, 1962.

These three books contain numerous poems all written by Japanese Haiku poets and translated by Mr. Beilenson (and Mr. Behn in Haiku Harvest). The books are small and contain very plain illustrations. As a source for Haiku, they are excellent.

Issa. A Few Flies and I. Selected by Jean Merrill and Ronnie Solbert. New York: Pantheon, 1969.

The collection of Japanese Haiku was all written by Japanese poet Issa who was born over two hundred years ago. The illustrations in this book are excellent and in the oriental fashion.

Johnson, Hannah Lyons. <u>Hello, Small Sparrow</u>. New York: Lothrop, Lee and Shepard, 1971.

This book contains delightful Haiku written in four lines instead of the popular three. The illustrations are wonderful in both black and white and color. They should be an inspiration to especially young children.

Lewis, Richard, ed. <u>The Moment of Wonder</u>. New York: Dial Press, 1964.

This book contains both Chinese and Japanese poetry and is illustrated by both Japanese and Chinese artists. While many Haiku poems are included, it is not the only form.

As a teacher, you may wish to find a copy of <u>Haiku in English</u> (Charles E. Tuttle Company, 1967, by Harold G. Henderson). It is an excellent little paperbound volume containing everything you will need to know about Haiku. The book is intended for teachers of native English speakers, but much of what is in the book is very valuable. Numerous lesson plans are given and most of them can be readily adapted for ESL. If you wish to do Haiku more extensively in your class, you will want to obtain this book.

Lee Bennett Hopkins in <u>Pass the Poetry, Please!</u> (Scholastic Books, Inc., 1972) also provides an excellent section on Haiku and other forms of oriental verse.

ESL students like to write their own versions of Haiku. The best way to begin this activity is to provide a nature-related experience in the class. The suggestions which follow give the stimuli necessary for writing Haiku.

Bring these items to class and display them in various places around the room.

1. Flowers in various stages of blooming with a dead or badly wilted flower.

2. An insect in a jar. Allow time for your students to study the object and then let the insect go.

3. A small bowl of dried leaves and a small bowl of new green leaves.

4. Rocks of all different shapes, sizes, and colors.

Since the students have already been given numerous examples of Haiku and have had many opportunities to reinforce the imagery, attempting to write their own Haiku is a natural extension. Below are samples of Haiku written by ESL students at the intermediate level.

The examples cited above were used as stimuli.

Flowers so beautiful
But they will die now
When you cut the flowers

Bee has to be free
In a bottle it will die
Sad for me and bee

Rocks are not alive
They look alive to me
Nice shapes and colors to see

Once alive and green
Now dead and brown in cup
Soon others like them, sad.

Give students an opportunity to share what they have written with other members of the class. Use the suggestions for sharing given previously in this chapter (p. 27). First have them share with the teacher, then put them in pairs, and then in small groups. Depending on your class, you may wish to have them share with the large group.

Students also like to find pictures for the poems they've written. Use old magazines and collected pictures as an in class activity for their personal poems as well.

Couplets

Language learners should also be introduced to traditional poetic form. The couplet is the simplest form of poetry which consists of two lines bound together by rhyme. Couplets have been used for centuries and are enjoyed by children and adults alike. They have often been used to teach moral principles and educational concepts like the Alphabet. If we think about it, we probably know many couplets already.

It is very easy to get your students to write short couplets. Have them brainstorm rhyming words and write them on the board in appropriate groups. After the brainstorming session, present simple couplets to the class with the last rhyming word left off:

I climbed the tree
The bird to _____.

```
My pet is a cat
and he is very _____.
```

(Written by ESL students)

Use the lists on the board to complete the couplets.
The first few couplets can be written. After that,
read the couplet and let them supply the last word
orally. After six or seven examples, have them try
to create their own couplets using the lists of rhyming
words on the board. An advanced level ESL class came
up with these couplets.

```
We failed the test!
You know the rest!

Hello and a smile
Makes me happy for awhile.

I like you it's plain to see.
Why won't you go out with me?
```

Give students a chance to share these couplets with
the class in the same way as described above, leaving
off the last rhyming word. They can do this in pairs
and small groups before they do it in front of the
entire class. Encourage them to talk, share and have
fun!

There are two forms of experimental verse which
have been used with great success in the ESL classroom. They are found poetry and concrete poetry.

Concrete Poetry

Concrete poems are picture poems made out of
letters and words. They are strongly visual, breaking

all traditional poetic forms. It is best illustrated
with the example below.

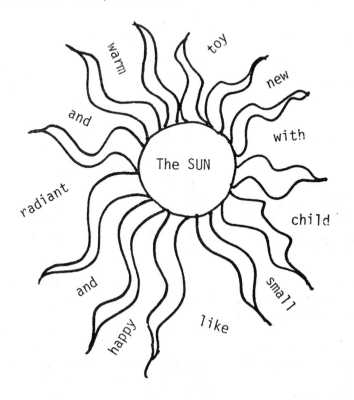

This particular example has worked well in a
number of classes. The Laugh Book (Scholastic Book
Services) by Ruth Belov Gross has three additional
examples which have worked well with young children
in ESL classes. Seeing these delightful examples
can also instill in you a desire to create your own
based on the needs and interests of your class.
Another interesting book I found was Street Poems by
Robert Froman. This book contains numerous examples
of concrete poetry and inspires teachers again to
create their own examples. The examples in the

Froman book are especially appropriate for children in urban areas since the content of the poetry relates to the city experience.

When introducing this poetic form, give an example, i.e., a sun. Have students draw their own sun and then write a poem as in the example. Some teachers prefer to provide the example and then have the students write their poem. Either way, teacher-produced or student-produced, can work depending on how much structuring your learners need to feel comfortable.

Students should have the opportunity to compare what they write and to share their poetry with the class. Later divide the class into small groups and give each group a new topic. Have them create their concrete poetry as a group and then share the results with the whole class.

Another diversion is to give each small group a different example and have each person work individually. Then, have them share in small groups.

If you have any difficulty thinking of examples to use, here are several ideas which have worked. Use your imagination. The idea is only the beginning. Concrete poetry is unique and may develop in any number of ways.

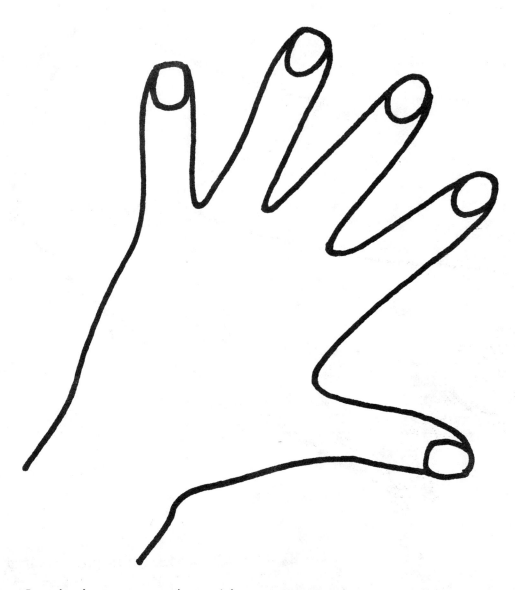

Permission to reproduce this page granted

Permission to reproduce this page granted

Permission to reproduce this page granted

Permission to reproduce this page granted

Permission to reproduce this page granted

Permission to reproduce this page granted

Found Poetry

Found poetry is poetry which just happens to be around. It could be things which are already written on menus, signs, or advertisements. Students enjoy looking for these things. Of course, they are not really writing poetry, but they are demonstrating their creativity and knowledge about the language and how it fits together, an essential part of the language learning process.

The example below may help in understanding what found poetry is and what students have done in creating these forms.

```
          P  I  C  T  U  R  E  S
                               P
                               I
                               C
(Child's Picture)              T
                               U
                               R
                               E
                               S
```

Send your film to us
No mess.
No fuss.

In this example the student found an advertisement
which caught her eye. She then arranged the words in
poetic form. Later, she added a small child posing
for a picture. Encourage your students to look for
"catchy" phrases or sentences and write them down.
They can arrange the phrases into poetic lines. Once
the ideas catch on, it is difficult to stop them!
Found poetry appears everywhere.

One student came up with this poetry after a visit
to the supermarket with an American friend.

        Z I P L O C*
            Ziploc

Zip it.
Lock it.

With ZipLoc
Heavy
Heavy duty
Heavy Duty Bags

    Z
      I
        P
          L
            O   *
              C

She had taken a striking phrase from the advertisement display, added to it, and arranged it in
poetic form. Then she had pasted colorful pictures
around it and enclosed the entire poem in a plastic
bag!

Two of the best resources for found poetry have
been Pop Poems by Ronald Gross (Simon & Schuster, 1967)

    ZipLoc* is a registered Trademark of the Dow Corning
        Company.

and an article in Elementary English (1971, pp. 1002-4) entitled "Found Poetry" by Myra Weiger. Both the book and the article contain numerous example poems from a variety of sources.

When introducing found poetry in the class, give a little explanation to the students. Show them examples of found poetry and turn them loose with coupons, magazines, paper, scissors, glue, etc., to create their own versions. Just make certain the materials you give them to work with are interesting and useful in their real-life situations. For example, a young male child of six or seven would not be interested in the same things as a middle-age female refugee. A book or catalogue on cars and things that go might be fun for the young boy while the immigrant woman might find a book on homes, plants or food more interesting.

Poetry can be used in a variety of ways in the classroom, from the published variety to student-created poems. What has been presented in the first three chapters only scratches the surface of possibilities. The best ideas come from the minds of creative and dedicated ESL teachers. Encourage your students to read, to write, to play around with the language and become comfortable with it, to use words in new and special ways, and to develop their own creative potential. Bringing ESL students and poetry together can be one of the most exciting experiences in a teaching career. Try some of the poetry activities in the following chapter and see!

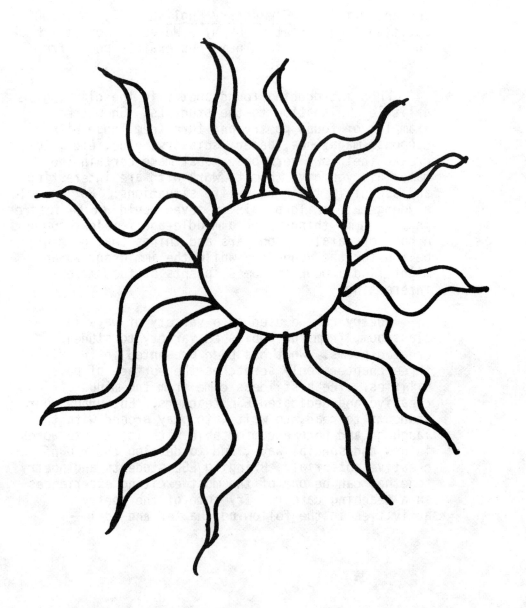

CHAPTER FOUR

Activities for the Classroom

CHAPTER FOUR
Activities for the Classroom

This chapter presents dozens of ideas for motivating poetry in ESL programs at all levels and age groups. However, very little attempt has been made to assign a specific age group or level to the individual activities since most of the activities can be adapted to fit the needs of most any group. Included in the activities are a variety of themes or topics which will tie-in with many areas of a curriculum. None of the activities involve excessive time or unusual materials. Collected items, items you just happen to have around, are more valuable than anything you can buy commercially. With imagination, creativity, and an occasional trip to the five-and-dime, you will have many successes in your classroom teaching English through poetry.

ACTIVITY #1

Title: "Handprint Poems"
Materials: Plain White Paper,
          liquid crayons
Level: Beginning, intermediate, advanced
Age group: Children, Young Adults

Give students plain white paper and liquid
crayons. Have them trace an outline of a hand on the
paper. Then ask the students to write a poem about
a hand using at least three of the words from the
list(s). If you've just finished working with couplets,
you might suggest writing only 2-line couplets.

Polish	Thumb
Fingers	Hand
Five	Three
Ring	Short
Fat	Me
Cat	See
Sing	Grand
Bank	Sand
Dumb	Nail

(Add any additional words you think would work or
delete any you think would not work with your class.)

Writing these questions on the board serves as a
stimulus to get them thinking:

1. Whose hand is this?
2. Why are hands important?
3. Have you ever hurt your hand?
4. Do you wear a ring?
5. Why do people wear rings?

After the poems have been written, give suggestions, if necessary, and have them recopy the poems on colored paper. Paste the poem on the outline of the hand they traced. If you have classroom space, make a bulletin board to display their work. Provide sharing time.

<u>Note</u>:

If you don't think your students would enjoy tracing their own hands, use the found poetry example on page 35.

ACTIVITY #2

Title: "Alphabet Poetry"
Materials Prepared letter handout
Level: Intermediate, advanced
Group: Children, Adults

Divide students into pairs or groups of three.
Give each pair or group a different letter of the
alphabet, e.g., t, b, s, g, m, etc. and have them
brainstorm as many words as they can beginning with
the letter given. Allow 5 minutes for brainstorming.
After the brainstorming session, tell them to write
a short sentence, limerick or tongue twister, using
as many of the words as possible. Some ESL students
at the advanced level wrote the tongue twisters
which follow.

> Margaret   and Mohammed Mahmoud's mother
>   matched in a magic music party in Miami.

> Stella and Susan Sorenson's sister, Sandra,
>   swam in the "Sunset" swimming pool on
>   Sunday at seven with her shiny silver
>   swimming suit!

> Danny and David Dickenson are going with
>   Droodle's Dad to Denver, driving a car
>   in December.

Give the students plenty of opportunity to share
their examples. If students are having difficulty
with certain sounds, give them those letters to
work on.

ACTIVITY #3

Title: "Mirrored Rhymes"
Materials: Bulletin board, class pictures,
          small mirror
Level: Intermediate, advanced
Group: Children, Adults

This is a good activity if you have a bulletin
board in your room or school. Place a small mirror
in the center of the board. Around the mirror put
some poems about mirrors. These can be published
poems or poems the students have written. For published poems you might consider the following:

"Mirror, Mirror!" by Deborah Ensign (in Richard
    Lewis' Miracles, Simon and Schuster, 1966)

"Phizzog" by Carl Sandburg (see anthology in
    this book)

Encourage students to write poems about mirrors if
they want to.

Entitle the bulletin board "Guess Who?"

Get each student to bring a picture, preferably
a childhood or baby picture to class for the display.
Place the pictures around the display. Under each
picture leave a space for students to write their
guesses about who's who. After two or three days,
take some time to find out who's who. Have students
share their ideas. Then find out from the students
when their picture was taken, how old they were, who
took the picture, etc.

A follow-up discussion on the ideas presented in
the poetry is also appropriate, focussing on individ-
uality and how we are all important and liked by

someone even though we all look different. We should
be happy with how we look. This follow-up activity
should be used with a class or group who know each
other quite well; otherwise, they may feel uncom-
fortable.

ACTIVITY #4

Title: "Shoe Song"
Materials: Plain white paper,
            liquid crayons
Level: Intermediate, Advanced
Group: Children

Have the children sit on the floor in a large
circle and ask them to take off one shoe and put it
in the middle of the circle. Focus their attention
on shoes and how different they all are. This is a
good opportunity to learn new vocabulary, e.g.,
tennis shoe, boot, sandal, oxford, sneaker, etc.
Review the vocabulary words by holding up the different shoes and having them respond or ask different
students to pick up the different types of shoes.
Find out answers to these questions:

Why do we wear shoes?
What is your favorite kind of shoes?
What color shoes do you like?
What kind of shoes do you wear to school?
What kind of shoes would you like to have?
(Add any other questions you feel appropriate.)

Allow plenty of time for sharing.

Have students take their own shoes from the circle
and return to a desk or table. Give each student a
plain piece of paper. Ask them to draw a shoe or
trace their foot, color it, and then write a short
poem about shoes. List the following vocabulary on
the board to help them.

Shoe	Oxford
Tennis Shoe	Sock
Toe	Boot
Heel	Polish

Shoelace	Foot
Sandal	Feet
Ked	Toes
Sole	Shiny
Worn	Dirty
Hole	Leather

Add any additional words they may need. Review any
difficult or unfamiliar vocabulary for them. Allow
small group sharing for the poetry and display their
poetry, if possible.

ACTIVITY #5

Title: "Painting Poems"
Materials: White paper, liquid crayons,
           water colors
Level: Intermediate, Advanced
Group: Children or Adults

Encourage students to draw or paint a picture
first and then find a poem that goes with it. Students
can also look for poems they feel appropriate for a
classmate's drawing. If they cannot find a suitable
poem, they may decide to write their own. In any case,
they have looked at a variety of poems, and been
exposed to a variety of language. Have plenty of
poetry books on hand. See resources in this book for
suggestions.

ACTIVITY #6

Title: "Pictures and Poems"
Materials: Pictures, Poetry books
Level: Intermediate, Advanced
Group: Children or Adults

Look into your personal picture file and post an interesting photograph or picture on a small bulletin board. Ask your students to look for poems they feel fit the mood of the poem or describe the illustration. Give the display a "catchy" title. For example, "Haunted Houses" under an illustration of an old house might elicit original poems or poems such as "The House at the Corner" by Myra Cohn Livingston (in Wide Awake and Other Poems, Harcourt, 1959). Post the poems when they write them or find them.

Other pictures and captions might deal with animals, nature, the environment, space, sports, or the sea.

Follow-up with an activity where the students share the poems they find.

ACTIVITY #7

Title: "Special Event"
Materials: Variable
Level: Intermediate, Advanced
Group: Children, Adults

Events in students' personal lives can encourage
the sharing of poetry. Birthdays, a new baby coming
into the family, or holiday celebrations can all be
perfect stimuli for writing poetry. Appropriate poems
can be selected or written, illustrated, and sent to
individuals celebrating extra special occasions.
Mother's Day, Father's Day, Valentine's Day and Christmas, of course, are ideal times to write and illustrate
greeting card verses for special friends and relatives.
Provide paper, glue, scissors, magazines, etc. for
students to make their own greeting cards. If they
don't want to write poetry, have them find a poem in
a book or simply have them write a short note/letter
or they can do both. Sometimes it is fun for students
to explain about a holiday to their families in their
home country. Even if they don't write poetry, they
are using the language to communicate something of
interest and importance. By looking for poetry to
include, they have been exposed to even more language.

ACTIVITY #8

Title: "Sensory Poetry"
Materials: Variable
Level: Beginning, intermediate,
        advanced
Group: Children, Adults

Language learners of all ages can be inspired to create poems after they have had a variety of planned sensory experiences. One way to motivate students to use their senses is to take them for several walks around the neighborhood or school. Be specific on each walk. Tell the class "Today we are going on a hearing walk to record sounds we hear," or "Today we are going on a smelling walk to record things we smell." On subsequent walks, learners can record all that they see, and so on. During each walk they should record all the various sounds they hear, sights they see, and so forth in a notebook or you can make a list for the bulletin board later. Visit areas never seen before.

Follow-up each walk or activity with writing time. Encourage them to write creatively about what they have experienced. Learners produce excellent writings when they are offered the opportunity to open up their senses. Beginners learn vocabulary and ideas quickly, and these ideas remain with them. They are not forgotten before the next class period.

ACTIVITY #9

Title: "Poetry Find"
Materials: Pocket board (see
            description below),
            poetry books
Level: Intermediate, advanced
Group: Children, Adults

Cut out several large pocket shapes from medium
weight cardboard or heavy paper. These pockets can
be painted with tempera paint or covered with fabric
patterns. Label each pocket with a category such as
The City, Insects, Animals or Me. Ask students to
write or find poems about these subjects.

Leave the bulletin board up for several weeks.
Remind the students everyday about the board. It is
a good idea to bring a poem to class every day which
fits one of the categories. Read the poem and have
the students tell you where it belongs. As students
find or write a poem, have them do the same thing.
When each student has contributed a poem, take some
extra time to review the poems and discuss where they
found the poem, why they like it, etc.

ACTIVITY #10

Title: "Lip Smackers"
Materials: Lipstick, colored paper
Level: Beginning, intermediate,
       advanced
Group: Children

This is a fun-filled activity for young children and needs to be supervised very closely. It is helpful to have someone to assist you if your class is very large.

Introduce the students to the poem "Whistle Wishes" by Barbara M. Hales (see anthology page 111).

Find out who can whistle in the room. Take time to listen to whistles. Introduce all the action-oriented vocabulary, i.e., pucker, blow, wiggle, etc. Provide little mirrors so they can see what they're doing with their lips. Have them repeat the poem after you and do what the poem suggests. Then move on to the next part of the activity.

All young children like to put on make-up. If children want to, have them paint their own lips with lipstick and then blot the lipstick on a piece of plain white paper to make the lip impressions. Have them do this until all the color is gone. For students who don't want to paint their lips, provide a paper with a lip outline. They can paint the outline on the paper and then blot in on a separate sheet in the same manner described above. When all students have a sheet of lips, have them copy "Whistle Wishes" from the black board. Display finished products. Return to the poem the next day. Find out if anyone has learned to whistle.

ACTIVITY #11

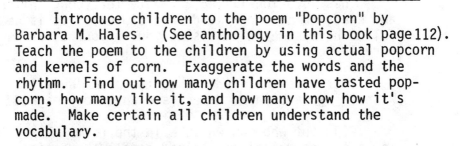

Title: Poetry's Poppin'
Materials: Electric frying pan,
          popcorn, oil, large cloth
Level: Beginning, intermediate,
       and advanced
Group: Children

Introduce children to the poem "Popcorn" by
Barbara M. Hales. (See anthology in this book page 112).
Teach the poem to the children by using actual popcorn
and kernels of corn. Exaggerate the words and the
rhythm. Find out how many children have tasted popcorn, how many like it, and how many know how it's
made. Make certain all children understand the
vocabulary.

Seat all children on the floor in a circle with
a large cloth and an electric frying pan in the middle.
Keep all children about five feet away from the pan.
Put oil and kernels in the pan and turn it on. Leave
the lid off. As the oil heats, the kernels will begin
to pop and the popcorn will pop out of the pan onto
the cloth. As the corn pops out, the children are
free to grab it and eat it.

After the kernels have popped, remove the pan.
Give the students time to tell you how they felt and
what they liked. Then find out how many can remember
the poem "Popcorn." Review it together again.
As a writing exercise, have them copy the poem and
glue a piece or pieces of popcorn to the sheet.
Display their work.

ACTIVITY #12

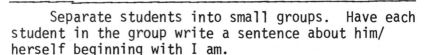

Title: "Group Poetry"
Materials: Writing paper
Level: Intermediate, Advanced
Group: Adults

Separate students into small groups. Have each student in the group write a sentence about him/herself beginning with I am.

> I am happy and sad.
> I am quiet sometimes.
> I am full of excitement.
> I am special.
> I am different.

Have the groups put all the sentences together in a list. This list of sentences can then be worked and reworked to create an original poem.

> Happy & sad,
> Full of excitement,
> Though lonely and quiet.
> Different?
> Special?
> Who knows?
> Just me.

This poem was written by an advanced level ESL group.

ACTIVITY #13

Title: "Famous Poets"
Materials: Variable
Level: Advanced
Group: Adults

Introducing a poet and his works can be stimulating and an excellent motivation for using the
library. Use a bulletin board or a large poster to
highlight the poet of the week. Change poets every
week. Assign one or two students to find out biographical information about the poet and have them
make a five minute presentation to the class. Provide
the biographical information on the bulletin board
and if possible, a photograph of the poet. If a
bulletin board is not available, use a large poster.
A poster can be moved and brought to class each day.
Assign two or three other students to find poetry by
the same poet and present it to the class.

Sometimes students like to write letters to the
poets themselves. If you have an address, encourage
them to do this. My students have often received
responses from the poet or the publisher, and this
makes it fun and interesting.

ACTIVITY #14

Title: "Poetry With Emotion"
Materials: Writing paper
Level: Intermediate, advanced
Groups: Adults

_____

Divide students into small groups. Write a
starter on the board like:

Anger is _____

_____

_____

_____

_____

Have each student in the group add a line. Other
starters could be:

Friends are . . . .
Peace is . . . .
America is . . . .
Happiness is . . . . . .

Have each group share their ideas. Discuss the
differences and similarities in responses. Change
starters and mix groups for variation.

ACTIVITY #15

Title: "Nouns"
Materials: Writing paper
Level: Intermediate, advanced
Group: Adults

Ask each student to think of a noun and to write
it down. Write an example on the blackboard, e.g.,
train. To the side write noun in parentheses. Go
around the room and have each person share their word.
This gives the teacher a chance to make certain everyone has understood and has chosen an appropriate word.
Next, have them write two adjectives to describe the
noun, e.g., speedy, noisy. Speedy and noisy describe
train. Write your example words on the board. To the
side write two adjectives. Then write three verbs
that the noun does, e.g., rumbles, clacks, roars.
Write the example words on the board and to the side
write three verbs. Then have them write a short feeling or comment, e.g., can't sleep. To the side write
short feeling. The last line should be a synonym for
the noun, e.g., bus on tracks. To the side write
synonym. Give them plenty of time to think and then
reflect. On the board you would have written:

        train (noun)
        speedy, noisy (two adjectives)
        rumbles, clacks, roars, (three verbs)
        can't sleep (short feeling)
        bus on tracks (synonym)

Check student work simultaneously as you proceed
through the exercise. Assist any student having
difficulty. Allow plenty of time for sharing. Have
students write their poems and display them on a
special poster. All students succeed in this exercise
and are left with positive feelings about poetry and
their language learning experiences.

ACTIVITY #16

Title: "Remembering"
Materials: Writing paper
Level: Intermediate, advanced
Group: Adults

Ask students to think about things which have
happened in their past life. Tell them you are going
to give them two or three minutes to simply think
and reflect on those past experiences. After this
reflective thinking, have them complete this phrase
in five different ways.

I remember . . . . . .

_____

_____

_____

_____

Give them plenty of time to write and collect their
thoughts. In small groups have them take turns
sharing what they have written. Later, return to a
large group and ask for volunteers to share their
thoughts with the class. Encourage other students
to ask questions about things they don't understand
or things they would like more information about.

ACTIVITY #17

Title: "Days"
Materials: Writing paper
Level: Beginning
Group: Adults

Divide students into small groups. Write the following phrase on the board:

A day in the life of . . . .

Each student should write one line which adds to the daily happenings in the life of a little boy, an immigrant, an old man, a housewife, etc. For example:

A day in the life of Jimmy.

He woke up.
He felt sad.
He got out of bed.

After each person has contributed encourage the group to work with their sentences to make certain they are correct. Have each group share what they have written.

ACTIVITY #18

Title: "Strip Poetry"
Material: Poetry chart,
          Strips of poetry
Level: Intermediate, advanced
Group: Children, Adults

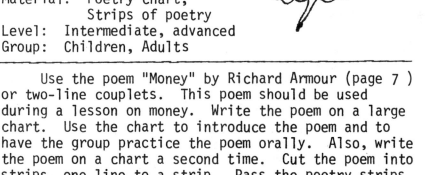

Use the poem "Money" by Richard Armour (page 7) or two-line couplets. This poem should be used during a lesson on money. Write the poem on a large chart. Use the chart to introduce the poem and to have the group practice the poem orally. Also, write the poem on a chart a second time. Cut the poem into strips, one line to a strip. Pass the poetry strips to the students. Have them memorize the strips. After two or three minutes take the strips away. Then have the class put the poem back together again orally. When they feel they are finished, have each person say their part in the correct order. The group should make corrections when there are mistakes. When they are satisfied, compare with the original poem.

Another version is to have them put the strips back in order by taping them to a large chart. Either way can be successful depending on the focus of your class. This exercise helps foster group co-operation.

ACTIVITY #19

Title: "Time"
Materials: Writing paper
Level: Intermediate, advanced
Age Group: Adults

Write the words <u>yesterday</u> and <u>today</u> on the black-board. The students should "brainstorm" things they <u>used to</u> do. Have them complete this sentence:

When I was . . . . . I used to . . . . .

After students have had time to think and share their answers, have them think about today, who they are and what they do. Then, they should complete this sentence:

Today I am . . . . . and I . . . . .

These two ideas can then be combined into poetic form. Some ESL students came up with these examples:

When I was young, I used to cry
but today I am older and I laugh instead.

When I was happy, I used to sing
but today I am sad and I work silently.

Give students plenty of opportunities to share and exchange ideas.

ACTIVITY #20

Title: "Future Wishes"
Materials: Blackboard or
          a large chart
Level: Beginning, intermediate
Age Group: Adults

This poetry activity can be done as a group. Begin with the phrase I wish . . . . Write the phrase on the board. Ask each student to think of a wish. Give them a few minutes to reflect. Go around the room and have each student add a part. If the class is large, divide it into smaller groups. Then together as a group, put the lines into poetic form. Use the exercise as a conversation starter. Find out why they want the wish, look at differences and similarities, etc.

ACTIVITY #21

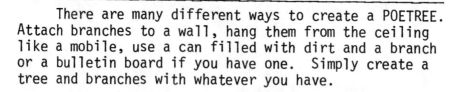

Title: "Poetree"
Materials: Large poster or bulletin
board, butcher paper,
liquid crayons, colored
construction paper
(shades of green)
Level: Beginning, intermediate, advanced
Age Group: Children, Adults

There are many different ways to create a POETREE.
Attach branches to a wall, hang them from the ceiling
like a mobile, use a can filled with dirt and a branch
or a bulletin board if you have one. Simply create a
tree and branches with whatever you have.

Ask the students to find their favorite poem and
copy it. Be certain to have them include their name
under the poem. Paste the copied poem on a piece of
green construction paper cut in the shape of a leaf.
Attach the leaf to the tree you have created. Add
pictures, if appropriate, and if you have them.

The POETREE can also be a seasonal tree. At
Christmas use Christmas poems, at Mother's Day,
Mother's Day poems, etc.

ACTIVITY #22

Title: "Poetry Zoo"
Materials: Pictures of animals
Level: Beginning, intermediate
       advanced
Age Group: Children, Adults

This activity is a great vocabulary builder.
Use a corner of the room to create a poetry zoo.
Hang pictures of animals on a bulletin board or from
a mobile attached to the ceiling. Ask students to
find or write poems about these animals, or ask
students to draw their favorite animal and find or
write a poem about it.

Spend time in the animal zoo reviewing the names
of the animals and giving students a chance to share
the poetry they have found or written.

ACTIVITY #23

Title: "Peek-a-boo" Poetry
Materials: Cardboard box,
          colored paper, glue
Level: Beginning, intermediate,
       advanced
Age Group: Children

Here is an activity that is perfect for children and capitalizes on their natural curiosity! Cover two shoe boxes with colored paper. In the first box, cut two small holes in one end. Inside, on the opposite end, paste a short poem. Have the children look through one tiny hole and shine a flashlight in the other hole to read the poem. Beside the box have a few short questions or a puzzler they must answer about the poem. Cut a hole in the top of the second box and use it as a deposit for answered questions or puzzlers. Adjust the content to fit the level you are working with.

ACTIVITY #24

Title: "Weather Poetry"
Materials: Poster, glue,
           weather poems
Level: Beginning, intermediate
       advanced
Age Group: Children, Adults

The weather is usually the focus of conversation
for a few minutes during each class period, so why
not capitalize on that and bring some "weather" poetry
into the class. Make a bulletin board or poster with
several different categories, e.g., "cloudy poems",
"sunny poems", "cold poems", "windy poems", etc. The
students can look for or write poems which fit the
different categories. (Try "Frost" by Barbara M.
Hales in the anthology in this book.) When the
bulletin board or poster has enough poems, the
students can select different poems to share with
the class. On a windy day, a student who selected a
"windy" poem can share that poem with the class.
You may want to help each student with the poem they
select. You'd be surprised how they always remember
their poems on the appropriate day!

ACTIVITY #25

Title: "Munching or Crunching"
Materials: Potato chips,
          5 different samples
          of snack foods
Level: Beginning, intermediate,
       advanced
Age Group: Children, Adults

Use Myra Cohn Livingston's poem "Street Song"
(page 5 this book).

Buy a large bag of potato chips. Divide your
students into small groups and prepare one small dish
of potato chips for each group. Seat students in
small groups on the floor or arrange the chairs in
circles.

Introduce "Street Song" on a large chart in front
of the group. Read the poem orally, exaggerate, play
around with it, have fun! Then tell the students
they are going to learn two new vocabulary words
"munching" and "crunching." Demonstrate crunching
and munching with a potato chip and ask the students
to follow or perhaps they can demonstrate for you.
Allow time for them to talk and have fun as each
group finishes their munching and crunching.

Prepare other snack foods for each group. Tell
the students to record the different tastes and
textures they experience. Practice the vocabulary
and discuss any questions that may arise.

An obvious point of departure would be snacking
customs, when and how we snack and why. Find out
about customs in their own countries if your
students come from multi-linguistic/multi-cultural
backgrounds.

ACTIVITY #26

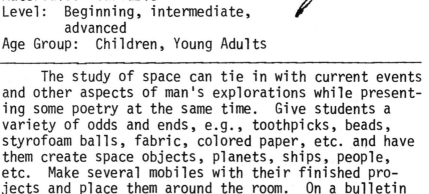

Title: "Science & Poetry"
Materials: Variable
Level: Beginning, intermediate,
        advanced
Age Group: Children, Young Adults

The study of space can tie in with current events
and other aspects of man's explorations while presenting some poetry at the same time. Give students a
variety of odds and ends, e.g., toothpicks, beads,
styrofoam balls, fabric, colored paper, etc. and have
them create space objects, planets, ships, people,
etc. Make several mobiles with their finished pro-
jects and place them around the room. On a bulletin
board make a student display of current events with
clippings on space exploration from newspapers and
magazines, original artwork and poetry. Include
several space poems. Face and Places: Poems For
You (Scholastic Book Services) has several good ones.
It is an inexpensive paperback book and well worth
the price.

ACTIVITY #27

Title: "Lost Poetry"
Materials: Mother Goose Rhymes, poster
            or bulletin board
Level: Intermediate, advanced
Age Group: Children

Pick several appropriate Mother Goose Rhymes, put them on a bulletin board with a picture. Ask appropriate questions depending on the rhymes you choose. Leave a space for children to write their responses.

1. What things are lost in these poems?
    (sheep, blackbirds, etc.)

2. What foods are mentioned?

3. What jobs are mentioned?

Change the question every few days. Review the answers and give children an opportunity to share.

ACTIVITY #28

Title: "Poetry Jar"
Materials: Two glass jars
Level: Intermediate, advanced
Age Group: Children

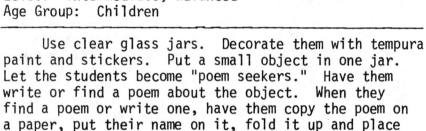

Use clear glass jars. Decorate them with tempura
paint and stickers. Put a small object in one jar.
Let the students become "poem seekers." Have them
write or find a poem about the object. When they
find a poem or write one, have them copy the poem on
a paper, put their name on it, fold it up and place
it in the second jar. Schedule a sharing time for
the poems.

ACTIVITY #29

Title: "Vocabulary Exercise"
Materials: Handout
Level: Advanced
Age Group: Adults

Poetry can be an effective stimulus for dis-
covering new vocabulary. Sometimes students need
extra help in understanding the poetic syntax. The
following activity was developed by Judy E. Winn-
Bell Olsen to assist her students in understanding
"The Road Not Taken" by Robert Frost (see page 111
in the anthology of this book).

For this exercise, students are paired and given
one copy of the poem and one copy of the exercise to
"encourage" them to collaborate. They are given up to
half an hour to work it through themselves (no
dictionaries allowed; arguing encouraged) before going
over it as a class. This certainly beats teacher
explanation and encourages independent learning. It
works well for any reading with a heavy new vocabulary
load.

Find words or phrases with these meanings:

1. one road divided into two and went in
    different directions (phrase)

2. woods having trees with yellow leaves (phrase)

3. because I wanted to walk on both roads at
    the same time (long phrase)

4. I stood for a long time (phrase)

5. one of the roads (word)

6. small bushes, branches, and plants in a woods (word)

7. which was as nice looking as the first one (phrase)

8. maybe it would be better for me (phrase)

9. having grass on it (word)

10. It was not used very much (phrase)

11. But really (phrase)

12. people walking on the roads (phrase)

13. the roads were almost equally used

14. the two roads (word)

15. Nobody had used the roads yet that day, because the leaves that had fallen on them were still yellow or green. (phrase)

16. I decided to walk on one road later. (sentence)

17. But I knew that roads continue and connect with others (phrase)

18. a long time from now (phrase)

19. fewer people have walked on this road (phrase)

20. walking on the less-traveled road (word)

21. my life is special because of it.

Follow-up with a discussion on a time when the student had a difficult decision to make. Discussion may also bring out some interesting cross-cultural points: one of Judy's Chinese students remarked that in Asian cultures, life would not be represented as a road, but as a river.

ACTIVITY #30

Title: "Poetic Imagery"
Materials: Writing paper
Level: Advanced
Age Group: Older Children, Adults

The idea of poetic imagery is a difficult concept for many language learners and yet most foreign students studying for a degree in higher education in the U. S. cannot help but be confronted with it. A simple exercise like this one may assist them in understanding this concept.

Use "Foot Blues" by Sydnie P. Cote in the anthology of this book, page 116 (or any poem you like which has good imagery).

Ask the students to begin by using the simile exercises outlined in Chapter 3. Gradually move them into understanding the imagery in the poem you choose. Explain that no one likes to have cold feet.

Ask questions

What are feet like when it's cold?
Feet are like _____.

What do they long to do?
They long to _____.

Follow-up with an oral reading of the poem. Discuss how feet feel when they are hot or cold. Encourage them to write poetry of their own.

ACTIVITY #31

Title: Poetry's Cookin'
Materials: Prepared question
            sheet
Level: Intermediate, advanced
Age Group: Children, Adults

Use the poem "Mummy Slept Late and Daddy Fixed Breakfast" by John Ciardi (see anthology page 105 in this book).

This poem can key a very interesting discussion on families. You might find out the following:

Who does the cooking in your family?
Can your father cook? Does he?
What do you usually have for breakfast?
What would you rather have for breakfast?
Have you ever fixed breakfast?

Include questions appropriate for your group. Prepare a sheet of questions. Have the students interview each other in pairs. Share the responses in large or small groups.

ACTIVITY #32

Title: "Mother Goose Village"
Materials: Variable
Level: Beginning, intermediate,
        advanced
Age Group: Children

   If you're working with young children, don't over-
look Mother Goose. These poems are popular with young
children because they like the rhythm, rhyme and
aliteration the poetry contains. The poetry is pleas-
ing to their ears.

   After your children are familiar with several
Mother Goose Rhymes, have them create a bulletin board
entitled a "Mother Goose Village." Have someone draw
"Jack's Corner," "King Cole's Court," "Mary's Garden,"
"Humpty Dumpty's Wall." If you don't have a permanent
classroom, have them use large charts which are portable
and can be moved and taken down. You won't need to
teach the rhymes because children will teach themselves
and learn from other children. The village provides
the stimulus, fun and excitement necessary!

ACTIVITY #33

Title: "Flower Garden Poetry"
Materials: Colored construction
            paper, white butcher or
            poster paper, glue,
            scissors
Level: Intermediate, advanced
Age Group: Children

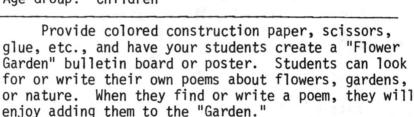

Provide colored construction paper, scissors, glue, etc., and have your students create a "Flower Garden" bulletin board or poster. Students can look for or write their own poems about flowers, gardens, or nature. When they find or write a poem, they will enjoy adding them to the "Garden."

For example:

> My garden is full of beautiful flowers
> It is a wonderful place
> To spend quiet hours.

ACTIVITY #34

Title: "Creative Dramatics "
Materials: Variable
Level: Intermediate, advanced
Age Group: Children

This is another activity which can be done when students are familiar with a variety of Mother Goose rhymes. Have the children act out the rhyme without words. The other children can try to guess the name of the rhyme depicted in the pantomime.

Some nursery rhymes which have worked especially well are:

Little Jack Horner
Little Miss Muffet
Wee Willie Winkie
Jack and Jill
Mary had a little lamb
Little boy blue
Old King Cole
Peter Peter

ACTIVITY #35

Title: "Creating Images"
Materials: Variable
Level: Intermediate, advanced
Age Group: Children, Adults

This activity has proven to be another good approach to encouraging language learners to write. Have them try to create images similar to the ones produced by poets. Hailstones and Halibut Bones by Mary O'Neill (Doubleday, 1961) is an excellent resource for this type of activity. It contains twelve poems about different colors. Each poem asks a question like "What is Gold?" "What is Black?" The poems tell about the color of objects and how colors make us feel, e.g., blue is sad, etc.

The poems also make students want to look at the colors around them and to do something about poetic imagery. Bring objects to class or make color charts where all things on the chart are blue, green, etc. Children can help look for the things to put on the charts. Encourage your students to make color images. Ask them "What color is this?" If they say yellow or red, say "Yellow like what?" or "Red like what?" They are then able to create their own images. Every student's response will be different!

You will be surprised at their creativity and ability to use the language.

ACTIVITY #36

Title: "Love Poems"
Material: Handout
Level: Intermediate, advanced
Age Group: Children, Adults

Have your students write a poem according to the following pattern.

> I love you because . . . . . .
> You make me feel . . . .
> When I . . . .

Example:

> Clouds.
> I love you because you are always
>   changing.
> You make me feel happy
> When I lie on my back and daydream.

Write the patterns on the board for the students to follow. Provide examples.

ACTIVITY #37

Title: "Feelings"
Materials: Handout
Level: Intermediate, advanced
Age Group: Adults

The introduction of poetry can be an excellent stimulus for students to discuss their feelings. As a class, make a list of feelings on the blackboard. You might ask, "How do you feel today?" or "What other feelings have you had?"

Ask each student to pick two feelings from the list and talk about the last time they had the feeling. For example,

> Happy.
> When my family called me.
>
> Sad.
> When I didn't get a letter.

Put students in small groups or pairs and have them share responses.

Follow-up with a poetry writing activity. Use a free-writing activity or the more structured one which follows.

> A Feeling . . . .
> When . . . .

Display the poetry on a bulletin board entitled "Feelings." Students also enjoy looking for poetry which describes feelings other people have.

ACTIVITY #38

Title: "Weekdays"
Materials: "Solomon Grundy" Poem
Level: Beginning, intermediate
Age Group: Children, Adults

Use the poem "Solomon Grundy" on page 121 in the anthology to get the students started. Introduce the poem in whatever manner you find comfortable. (See Chapter One, Using Poetry in ESL, for suggestions). Ask the students to substitute things which have happened in their past week for things which happened to Solomon Grundy.

For example:

Solomon Grundy got no letters on Monday
Still no on Tuesday
No on Wednesday.
Asked on Thursday
Told no on Friday
Feel bad on Saturday
Cry on Sunday
Got no letters
Poor Solomon Grundy.

(Uncorrected. By an intermediate level ESL Student)

This is a good easy way to find out what has been happening in their week in a non-threatening way. In addition, students learn days of the week, new verbs, and new past tense forms.

CHAPTER FIVE

Readers Theatre

CHAPTER FIVE
Readers Theatre

Introduction

Readers Theatre is one of the most popular forms
for presenting literature of any kind for oral interpretation. Poetry, letters, essays, and similar
selections may be successfully adapted. Since
Readers Theatre does not require the use of expensive
costumes, scenery, or props, it is also suitable for
classroom presentation and has been used with great
success in a number of ESL classes.

The idea of using Readers Theatre in ESL is
relatively new. It is especially appropriate, however, because with Readers Theatre, students are free
to use a variety of materials such as their own
poems, essays, pictures, music, etc., and produce
their own scripts. This provides an opportunity for
the students to become involved and to use the
language in creative and meaningful ways. While
poetry, both published and student created, most
frequently comprises the "core" of the Readers
Theatre script, it is by no means the only thing
students make use of in selecting their program.
You will be pleasantly surprised at their creativity!
Not only does Readers Theatre give them a chance to
use their new language in writing their own script,
but all original scripts are subsequently practiced

and presented before a small audience, so they have more of an opportunity to develop their oral communicative skills.

This chapter will introduce you to Readers Theatre by outlining a brief history of its development and reviewing its value as a language teaching device. Suggestions for preparing original scripts and presenting them before a small audience are also given. In order to demonstrate the feasibility and practicality of these ideas, two original scripts by ESL students are also included. While you may not necessarily use these scripts in your classes (although you can, but your students will probably want to write their own) they should inspire you as to what students can do when given encouragement and the opportunity to be creative.

A Brief History

The revival of Readers Theatre in modern times is comparatively recent, but as a form of oral art it is not completely new. The roots of Readers Theatre can be traced to the dramatic practices of fifth-century B. C. Greece, where wandering minstrels known as "rhapsodes" spoke recitative portions of national epics. These were often read to the accompaniment of a lyre and many times a second reciter would be included, conveying a form of dialogue between two characters (Bahn, 1932).

Similar interpretative reading was also evident in Medieval times. The church liturgy was amplified by the addition of symbolic costume, suggestion of dialogue and mimetic action. The Easter trope eventually became a chanted colloquy between voices of the choir which signified the two Marys and a responding angel (Schelling, 1925).

Readers Theatre in the United States was evident as early as the 1890's. Private groups assembled specifically for the purpose of reading whole plays or selected scenes. Each individual read the part of a single character. The parts were often committed to memory and conveniently executed from a sitting position (Mattingly and Crimes, 1970).

Although these early readings were representative of Readers Theatre technique and style, the term itself was not used until 1945. A New York professional group staged a production of Oedipus Rex (Nathan, 1946). Oedipus Rex itself was not a critical success, but it was followed closely by Don Juan in Hell in 1951 and John Brown's Body in 1952. Although entirely different in their presentations, both of these productions were successful and marked a critical beginning to a new dramatic movement.

Readers Theatre is basically experimental. In the ESL classroom there are no set rules on staging technique or approach. The students are free to be themselves, to do what seems right to them. They may wish to use stools and have their scripts on lecterns or they may have their scripts memorized and may move freely about the room. The scope of materials is also limitless; scripts vary greatly in theme and literature or materials. These diverse possibilities in staging techniques, theme, and materials, encourage energetic experimentation. It also provides students with a sounding board wherein they can voice their private concerns and feelings about a wide variety of topics. As you read through the two original scripts, you will notice how they have become vehicles for the students to voice these opinions and concerns.

Preparing Original Scripts

1. It is usually best for the teacher to select a topic for the group and to set a time limit for the presentation. Students should be able to choose their own groups.

2. Set a time table for the students. Decide when outlines and rough drafts should be submitted and when they should schedule a short conference with you. Require an outline first.

3. Have plenty of resource material available for the students, i.e., books, records, poster paper, etc.

4. Suggest several selections the students can use as "core" pieces. Usually this is poetry.

5. Demonstrate a few staging techniques. Show them how they can sit on the stools, turn around, etc. The teacher is always free to give suggestions. If the teacher helps them get started, they can usually work from there.

REFERENCES

Bahn, Eugene. "Interpretative Reading in Ancient Greece." Quarterly Journal of Speech. 18 (June 1932) : 434-437

Coger, Leslie Irene and Melvin R. White, Readers Theatre Handbook. 2nd ed. Glenview, Illinois: Scott, Foresman and Company, 1974.

Mattingly, Aletha Smith, and Wilm H. Grimes. Interpretation: Writer, Reader, Audience. 2nd ed. Belmont, California: Wadsworth Publishing Company, Inc., 1970.

Nathan, George Jean. The Theatre Book of the Year: 1945-46. New York: Alfred A. Knopf, Inc. 1946.

Schelling, Felis. Elizabethan Playwrights. New York: Harper and Row Publishers, 1925.

Original Readers Theatre
Script #1
"Americans"

Reader #1:   Who are Americans?

Reader #2:   They are.

Reader #3:   Black

Reader #4:   White

Reader #2:   Chinese

Reader #5:   Japanese

Reader #3:   American Indians

Reader #4:   They are people.

Reader #1:   "E Pluribus Unam"
             (written on a sign)

Reader #5:   Latin for "out of many, one"
             Out of all these people. . . . . .

(Other readers murmur softly White, Japanese, Black,
Chinese)

             Have come one people, Americans.

Reader #1:   And yet, who are Americans?

Reader #2:   We'd like to talk about Americans in four
             separate categories.

             English Immigrants
                 (sign)

Reader #3:   American Indians
                  (sign)

Reader #5:   Afro-americans
                  (sign)

Reader #1:   Later immigrants
                  (sign)

Reader #2:   Great Britain or England was the country
                  who most influenced the history and
                  culture of early America, known then as
                  the colonies. The colonies didn't like
                  England because of taxes.

                  (Folk Song: "The Tea Party")

                  Tea-ships near to Boston lying,
                  On the wharf a numerous crew.
                  Sons of Freedom never dying,
                  Then appeared in view!

                  Chorus:
                  With a rink-tum, dink-tum,
                  Fa la link-tum, then appeared in view,
                  With a rink-tum, dink-tum,
                  Fa la link-tum, then appeared in view!

                  Armed with hammers, axes, chisels,
                  Weapons new for war-like deed,
                  Toward the tax-ed, freighted vessels
                  On they came with speed.

                  Chorus:
                  With a rink-tum, dink-tum,
                  Fa la link-tum, on they came with speed.
                  (2 times)

Overboard she goes my boys, ho,
Where darkling waters roar;
We love our cup of tea full well but
Love our freedom more.

Chorus
With a rink-tum, dink-tum,
Fa la link-tum, love our freedom more.
(2 times)

Deep, into the sea descended
Cursed weed of China's coast;
Thus at once our fears were ended,
Rights shall ne'er be lost!

Chorus:
With a rink-tum, dink-tum,
Fa la link-tum, rights shall ne'er be lost!
(2 times)

Reader #1: They also sang other songs. One of the
            most popular was this song "Yankee Doodle."

Reader #4: The song was originally sung by the British
            to poke fun at the Americans. After
            Lexington & Concord the Americans made
            their own song. It went like this.

"Yankee Doodle

Yankee Doodle went to town.
Riding on a pony.
Stuck a feather in his hat
And called it Macaroni.

CHORUS:
Yankee Doodle keep it up,
Yankee Doodle dandy.
Mind the music and the step,
And with the girls be handy.

Father and I went down to camp,
Along with Captin Goodin',
And there we saw the men and boys
As thick as has-ty pudd-din'.

CHORUS

Reader #3: Eventually the colonies became free from England, but the English influence would remain.

Reader #5: American Indians have also influenced the history and culture of the United States.

Reader #1: When the first white people came to America, the Indians were already here. They had their own cultures and customs.

Reader #2: The white people thought they lived in strange houses
(A large picture of a teepee)

Reader #3: and they wore strange clothes.
(A large picture of 4 Indians)

Reader #1: And yet, they were the Americans. But no matter how different, Americans are trying to accept each other.

Reader #5: "Phizzog" by Carl Sandburg
(p.120in the anthology of the book)

Reader #4: Afro-Americans are the next group. They were brought from Africa as slaves. They have suffered inequality.

Reader #2: (Poem by Laugston Hughes, black poet, excerpt lines taken from Life, Liberty and the Pursuit of Happiness p. 77 .)

Reader #1:   Laugston Hughes was a black poet who wrote
             about the black experience. He and many
             black leaders began to make others see
             their injustices.

Reader #3:   Immigrants continued to come to the U. S.,
             but in later years they were mostly from
             Latin America (Cuba, Mexico, and Puerto
             Rico) and from Indochina.

Readers: I may be black
             I may be white
             My color is not important.

             I am an American.

Choral Reading: ("Different Faces" by Eve Merriam,
                  Faces and Places: Poems for You,
                  Scholastic Book Services, 1971,
                  p. 7.)

Notes:

     These students were just completing a course in
American Culture. Many of the ideas they developed in
their script had been discussed previously in class.
The textbook for the course was Life, Liberty and the
Pursuit of Happiness by Mary Ann Kearny and
(Newbury House Publishers, 1979) It was responsible
for the organization of much of the materials (see
Chapter 2). The songs "The Tea Party" and "Yankee
Doodle" were also taught in their class. One of the
Thai students played the guitar for the songs. Because
we had had such fun with the songs in class, the
students felt very comfortable with them.

     The poetry was of their own choice and surprised
even the teacher! Illustrations were drawn by one of
the group members and greatly enhanced the presentation.

Colorful pictures from magazines would have worked just as well.

For this presentation, the students used stools and lecterns for the scripts. This gave them more confidence. Scripts always remained on the lecterns. When the readers switched stools, they always had a script in front of them.

Original Readers Theatre
Script #2

Reader #1: Most Americans like animals. We are surprised that so many Americans have pets. The most popular pets we think are cats.
(Large picture of cats)

Reader #2: ("The Kitten" by Carl Sandburg. See p. 9.)

Reader #3: ("Tracks in the Snow" by Margaret Hillert)

Reader #4: Many Americans have dogs for pets, but we hear most people complain about their "pups." They do many things which make it hard for their owners.
(Large picture of a dog)

Reader #1: ("Puppy" by Lee Bennett Hopkins)

Readers #2, (Choral Reading of "An Introduction
#3, #4: to Dogs" by Ogden Nash)

Reader #1: Sometimes people have strange pets.

Readers #1, (Choral Reading of "The Ant Village"
#2, #3: by Marion Edey and Dorothy Grider)

Reader #4:   One American told me that she had a bird
               in her yard every morning. Although the
               bird was wild, it seemed like a pet
               because it was there everyday.

Reader #3:   ("Owls Aren't So Smart" by Richard Shaw)

Reader #2:   Sometimes people consider wild animals as
               pets. Old Jake Sutter does.

Reader #1:   ("Old Jake Sutter" by Kaye Starbird)

Reader #3:   Many people have many different kinds of
               pets. We all agree, however, that there
               is one pet none of us would want to have.

Reader #2   (Choral Reading "The Black Snake" by
   and #4:   Patricia Hubbell)

Note:

    All the poems in this script were taken from a
small anthology entitled Potato Chips and a Slice
of Moon selected by Lee Bennett Hopkins and Misha
Arenstein (Scholastic Book Inc. 1976).

CHAPTER SIX

Anthology for ESL

CHAPTER SIX
Anthology for ESL

Included in this short anthology are poems which have been used successfully in ESL classes with children and adults and with varying levels from beginning to advanced. They differ in subject matter and format so that students are exposed to the widest range of poetry possible. For many of the poems, activities have already been provided. (See Chapter 4, Activities for the Classroom). Others are waiting for your imagination and creativity to bring them to life! Have fun with these poems. They are to enjoy, to bring laughter and fun to your classes, and to touch your students in perhaps a different way. May they bring as much of what is good about language learning to your classes as they have brought to mine!

Childhood Things

MUMMY SLEPT LATE AND
DADDY FIXED BREAKFAST

Daddy fixed the breakfast.
He made us each a waffle.
It looked like gravel pudding.
It tasted something awful.

"Ha, ha," he said, "I'll try again.
This time I'll get it right."
But what I got was in between
Bituminous and anthracite.

"A little too well done? Oh well,
I'll have to start all over."
That time what landed on my plate
Looked like a manhole cover.

I tried to cut it with a fork:
The fork gave off a spark.
I tried a knife and twisted it
Into a question mark.

I tried it with a hack-saw.
I tried it with a torch.
It didn't even make a dent.
It didn't even scorch.

The next time Dad gets breakfast
When Mommy's sleeping late,
I think I'll skip the waffles.
I'd sooner eat the plate!

                    - John Ciardi

                 DRINKING FOUNTAIN

When I climb up
  To get a drink
It doesn't work
  The way you'd think.

I turn it up.
  The water goes
And hits me right
  Upon the nose.

I turn it down
  To make it small
And don't get any
  Drink at all.

                    - Marchette Chute

THE CITY MOUSE
AND THE GARDEN MOUSE

The city mouse lives in a house;
　The garden mouse lives in a bower,
He's friendly with the frogs and toads,
　And sees the pretty plants in flower.

The city mouse eats bread and cheese;
　The garden mouse eats what he can;
We will not grudge him seeds and stalks,
　Poor little, timid, furry man.

- Christina Georgina Rossetti

FIVE LITTLE CHICKENS

Said the first little chicken,
With a queer little squirm,
"Oh, I wish I could find
A fat little worm!"

Said the next little chicken,
With an odd little shrug,
"Oh, I wish I could find
A fat little bug!"

Said the third little chicken,
With a sharp little squeal,
"Oh, I wish I could find
Some nice yellow meal!"

Said the fourth little chicken,
With a small sigh of grief,
"Oh, I wish I could find
A green little leaf!"

Said the fifth little chicken,
With a faint little moan,
"Oh, I wish I could find
A wee gravel-stone!"

"Now, see here," said the mother,
From the green garden-patch,
"If you want any breakfast,
You must come and scratch."

THE KITTEN PLAYING WITH
THE FALLING LEAVES

See the kitten on the wall
Sporting with the leaves that fall!
Withered leaves, one, two and three,
From the lofty elder-tree.
Through the calm and frosty air
Of this morning bright and fair
Eddying round and round they sink
Softly, slowly.--One might think,
From the motions that are made,
Every little leaf conveyed
Some small fairy, hither tending,
To this lower world descending.
--But the kitten how she starts!
Crouches, stretches, paws, and darts:
First at one, and then its fellow,
Just as light, and just as yellow:
There are many now--now one--
Now they stop and there are none.
What intentness of desire
In her up-turned eye of fire!
With a tiger-leap half way,
Now she meets the coming prey.
Lets it go at last, and then
Has it in her power again.

- William Wordsworth

MY FRIEND

I have a special friend named Sue;
She likes to do the things I do.
We share a lot of secret talk,
But sometimes we just think and walk.

And though our looks are not the same
And though my name is not her name,
It seems my thoughts are her thoughts too.
That's how it is with friends like Sue!

I think that when the world was planned
And little girls were in demand,
Heavenly Father somehow knew
I'd need a friend; so He sent Sue.

- Barbara M. Hales

WHISTLE WISHES

I pucker my lips,
Then I blow and I blow.
I look in the mirror
To get them just so.
My lip muscles twitch
And my breath comes out fast,
But there's no sort of whistle
That goes sliding past.
I wiggle my tongue
Into various places,
But all that I make
Are ridiculous faces.
I'll never give up though.
My mouth's pretty clever.
I know that my whistle
Can't hide there forever.

                    - Barbara M. Hales

POPCORN

Pippity pop
Skippety-skop
The kernels are pushing
   their way to the top
And once I start eating-
I know I won't stop!

- Barbara M. Hales

MY TOES

My toes seldom speak
  except to say eek!
At the feel of frost on their fannies.

I have heard them moan
  and give out a groan
When stubbed in a dark nook or cranny.

Sometimes they are bruised,
  overused and abused
But they'd never change places with Danny's.

                - Kim Christison

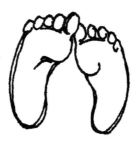

Everyday Things

TAKING OFF

The airplane taxis down the field
And heads into the breeze,
It lifts its wheels above the ground,
It skims above the trees,
It rises high and higher
Away up toward the sun,
It's just a speck against the sky
--And now it's gone!

-Anonymous

Ignore dull days; forget the showers;
Keep count of only shining hours.

-Anonymous

THIS IS JUST TO SAY

I have eaten
the plums
that were in
the icebox

and which you were probably
saving
for breakfast

Forgive me
they were delicious
so sweet
and so cold.

                - William Carlos Williams

FOOT BLUES

Crystal and sapphire gems
  wrapped in wool,
silver and cobalt ice toes
  crunching on frostbitten snow,
longing to thaw
  to azure and ivory
and caper barefoot
  on melted turquoise.

                    - Sydnie P. Cote

FROST

The frost
  on hanging bough appears
As weeping willow's
  frozen tears.

                    - Barbara M. Hales

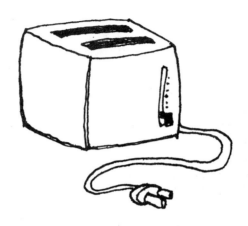

THE TOASTER

A silver-scaled Dragon with jaws flaming red
Sits at my elbow and toasts my bread.
I hand him fat slices, and then, one by one,
He hands them back when he sees they are done.

        - William Jay Smith

ACCIDENTALLY

Once--I didn't mean to,
but that
was that--
I yawned in the sunshine
and swallowed a gnat.

I'd rather eat mushrooms
and bullfrogs' legs,
I'd rather have pepper
all over my eggs

than open my mouth
on a sleepy day
and close on a gnat
going down that way.

It tasted sort of salty.
It didn't hurt a bit.
I accidentally ate a gnat.
and that
was
it!

- Maxine W. Kumin

CAT

A cat, black, and fat
Napped on my lap
Just some fur, a purr
An occasional stir.
He blinked wide awake
At the sound of the door
And quietly left
To be seen no more.

- Kim Christison

PHIZZOG

This face you got,
This here phizzog you carry around,
You never picked it out for yourself,
   at all, at all--did you?
This here phizzog--somebody handed it
   to you
   am I right?
Somebody said, "Here's yours, now go
   see what you can do with it."
Somebody slipped it to you and it was
   like a package marked:
"No goods exchanged after being taken
   away"--
This face you got.

                    -Carl Sandburg

SOLOMON GRUNDY

Solomon Grundy was born on a Monday
Christened on Tuesday
Married on Wednesday
Took ill on Thursday
Worse on Friday
Died on Saturday
Buried on Sunday
And that was the end of Solomon Grundy!

- Nursery Rhyme

TONGUE TWISTERS

You've no need to light a night light
On a light night like tonight,
For a night light's light's a slight light,
And tonight's a night that's light.
When a night's light, like tonight's light,
It is really not quite right
To light night lights with their slight lights
On a light night like tonight.

- Anonymous

I eat my peas with honey,
I've done it all my life,
It makes the peas taste funny,
But it keeps them on my knife.

- Anonymous

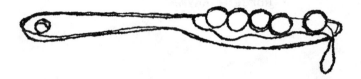

FAITH IS A FINE INVENTION

Faith is a fine invention
For gentlemen who see;
But microscopes are prudent
In an emergency.

- Emily Dickinson

WINTER SEASON

Deep in the mountains we have no calendar
To tell us when the seasons change.
Flowers bloom--we guess that it is spring;
Leaves fall, so it is autumn.

And when children hunt for warm clothes,
We know it must be winter!

- Anonymous

Love & Life & Things

THE ROAD NOT TAKEN

Two roads diverged in a yellow wood,
And sorry I could not travel both
And be one traveler, long I stood
And looked down one as far as I could
To where it bent in the undergrowth;

Then took the other, as just as fair,
And having perhaps the better claim,
Because it was grassy and wanted wear;
Though as for that the passing there
Had worn them really about the same,

And both that morning equally lay
In leaves no step had trodden black.
Oh, I kept the first for another day!
Yet knowing how way leads on to way,
I doubted if I should ever come back.

I shall be telling this with a sigh
Somewhere ages and ages hence:
Two roads diverged in a wood, and I--
I took the one less traveled by,
And that has made all the difference.

- Robert Frost

GENTLE PRAYER

A gentle prayer is what I'll say
To close this peaceful, gentle day.

With gratitude that I have heard
The pre-dawn chirpings of a bird.

With thankfulness that I have seen
The many hues of summer-green.

With singing heart that I could feel
The soft warm grasses when I kneel.

With love for those who give me care
I softly close my gentle prayer.

- Barbara M. Hales

TODAY

Today is a day
That exists for the simple reason
that it is today.

Today is a time
Vitally here and now, justified
because it is, here and now.

Today is a moment
That will never be again--And never was
   there ever
a moment such as this.

And because today
Was the day on which
I discovered I loved you.

Tomorrow is justified.

- Roger E. W. B. Olsen

ON HURRYING

It's hurry to bed, and it's hurry to rise.
It's hurry to dress, wipe the sleep from
  your eyes.
It's hurry to school, and hurry straight
  home.
I'm supposed to hurry when I need to roam.
How can you hurry to watch butterflies?
And can you look fast at bright evening skies?
How can you rush, watching bugs crawl and
  climb?
And hurrying to sleep leaves no happy-thought
  time.
I'm puzzled with grown-ups who hurry so fast.
Don't they know lots of wonderful things can
  slip past?
So I hurry quite slowly when nobody sees,
Taking time to look long at the creatures
  in trees.
I run, not too quickly, when whippoorwills
  sing;
I never go fast, slowing down in my swing.
And I pray slowly, talking with Father above.
It takes time to be grateful, to feel and
  to love.

- Barbara M. Hales

SOMETIMES

Sometimes
I want
To crawl
into my
own private
little hole

And then I'll cover myself
With my eyelids.

- Roger E. W. B. Olsen

CHAPTER SEVEN

Resources

CHAPTER SEVEN
Resources

GENERAL RESOURCES

All listed elsewhere in this publication

Aldis, Dorothy. The Secret Place and Other Poems. Scholastic Book Services.

Alexander, Arthur. The Poet's Eye: An Introduction to Poetry for Young People. Prentice-Hall. Englewood Cliffs, New Jersey.

Beilenson, Peter. Japanese Haiku. Translated. The Peter Pauper Press, 1956.

Beilenson, Peter. The Four Seasons. The Peter Pauper Press, 1956.

Beilenson, Peter and Harry Behn. Haiku Harvest. The Peter Pauper Press.

Froman, Robert. Street Poems. McCalls, 1971.

Gross, Ruth Belov. The Laugh Book. Scholastic Book Services.

Gross, Ronald. Pop Poems. Simon and Schuster, 1967.

Christison, Mary Ann. "Incorporating Poetry in ESL" in Cross Currents Vol. VII. No. 2.

Hales, Barbara. The Elf in My Ear. The Blue Creek Press, 1978.

Henderson, Harold G. Haiku in English. Charles E. Tuttle Company, 1967.

Hopkins, Lee Bennett and Mish Arenstein. Faces and Places: Poems for You. Scholastic Books, Inc. 1971.

Hopkins, Lee Bennett. <u>Pass the Poetry, Please!</u>
    Scholastic Books, Inc. 1972.

Hopkins, Lee Bennett and Misha Arenstein. <u>Potato Chips</u>
    <u>and a Slice of Moon</u>. Scholastic Books, Inc. 1976.

Johnson, Hannah Lyons. <u>Hello, Small Sparrow</u>.
    Lothrop, Lee and Shephard, 1971.

Lewis, Richard. <u>The Moment of Wonder</u>. Dial Press, 1964.

Lewis, Richard. <u>Miracles</u>. Simon and Schuster, 1966.

Livingston, Myra Cohn. <u>Wide Awake and Other Poems</u>.
    Harcourt, 1959.

Merrill, Jean and Ronnie Solbert. <u>A Few Flies and I</u>.
    Pantheon, 1969.

O'Neill, Mary. <u>Hailstones and Halibut Bones</u>.
    Doubleday, 1961.

Schaefer, Charles and Kathleen C. Miller, eds.
    <u>Young Voices</u>. Bruce Publishing Co., 1971.

Walter, Nina Willis. <u>Let Them Write Poetry</u>. Holt,
    Rhinehart and Winston, 1962.

Weiger, Myra. "Found Poetry" in <u>Elementary English</u>.
    1971. pages 1002-4.

SOURCES OF EDUCATIONAL MATERIALS CITED

Alemany Press, Ltd., P. O. Box 5265, San Francisco,
   CA 94101

Atheneum Publishers, 122 East 42nd Street, New York,
   N. Y. 10017

Blue Creek Press, P. O. Box 375, Brigham City, UT 84302

Bruce Publishing Co., c/o MacMillan & Co., 866 3rd Ave.,
   New York, N. Y. 10022

Citation Press, 50 West 44th St., New York, N. Y. 10036

Crowell (Thomas Y.) Company, 600 Fifth Ave., New York,
   N. Y. 10022

Collier & MacMillan, Inc., 866 Third Ave., New York,
   N. Y. 10022

Delacorte Press, 750 Third Ave., New York, N. Y. 10017

Dell Publishing Company, Inc., 750 Third Ave., New York,
   N. Y. 10017

Dial Press, Inc., 750 Third Ave., New York, N. Y. 10017

Doubleday and Company, Inc., 277 Park Ave., New York,
   N. Y. 10017

Dutton (E. P.) & Company, 201 Park Ave. South, New York,
   N. Y. 10003

Farrar, Straus & Giroux, Inc., 19 Union Square West,
   New York, N. Y. 10003

Harcourt, Brace, Jovanovich, 757 Third Avenue, New York,
   N. Y. 10017

Harper & Row, Publishers, 10 East 53rd St., New York, N. Y. 10022

Holt, Rinehart and Winston, Inc., 383 Madison Ave., New York, N. Y. 10017

Lippincott (J. B.) Co., East Washington Sq., Philadelphia, PA 19105

Little, Brown & Co., Inc., 34 Beacon St., Boston, MA 02106

Lothrop, Lee and Shepard Co., Inc., 105 Madison Ave., New York, N. Y. 10016

McCall Books, 230 Park Ave., New York, N. Y. 10017

Macmillan Co., 866 Third Ave., New York, N. Y. 10022

McGraw-Hill Book Company, 330 West 42nd St., New York, N. Y. 10036

National Council of Teachers of English, 1111 Kenyon Road, Urbana, IL 61801

New Direction Publishing Co., c/o W. W. Norton, 500 Fifth Ave., New York, N. Y. 10010

Pantheon Books, 201 East 50th St., New York, N. Y. 10022

Peterson, Kathy, #2 Walden Road, Ephraim, UT 84627

Prentice-Hall, Inc., Englewood Cliffs, NJ 07632

Putnam's (G. P.) Sons, 200 Madison Ave., New York, N. Y. 10016

Rand McNally & Co., Box 7600, Chicago, IL 60680

Scholastic Book Services, 50 West 44th St., New York,
    N. Y. 10036

Simon and Schuster, 630 Fifth Ave., New York,
    N. Y. 10036